Ogre Jokes

Q. Why don't ogres eat rich kids?
A. Because they're spoiled.

Q. Why did the dragon get fat?
A. Because it was an ogre-eater.

Q. Which beans do ogres like to munch?
A. Human beans.

Q. What's the difference between boogers and brussels sprouts?
A. Ogres won't eat brussels sprouts.

X-treme Eating

If becoming a pro athlete seems beyond your reach, train your stomach for victory instead.

In April 2008, when Patrick "Deep Dish" Bertoletti was just 23 years old, he became the world's oyster-eating champion after downing 34 dozen raw oysters in eight minutes. He also challenged "Locust" LeFevre's pickled jalapeño record in 2008 (he ate 191 in 6½ minutes), but didn't beat it. He graduated from college with a degree in—what else—culinary arts!

Toad Tongue Tanglers

One word has been removed from each of these tongue twisters, which you need to put back in.

Once you've done that, try saying each one three times fast.

A. MARRIED	**D.** ANKLES	**G.** TOLD
B. PLUNGERS	**E.** BERT	**H.** ELEGANT
C. JEN'S	**F.** CHOKE	**I.** TIP-TOP

1. PLASTIC _____ UNPLUG FASTER.
2. JOHN JOINED _____ GYM.
3. MARLY _____ EARLY.
4. BIG _____ BURPED.
5. _____ ELEPHANT.
6. _____ KID-TOPIA.
7. UNCLE'S _____.
8. TOAD _____.
9. CROAK _____.

Did you know? A group of toads is called a *knot*.

Answers

Toad Tongue Tanglers
1. B 2. C 3. A 4. E 5. H
6. I 7. D 8. G 9. F

Fart Facts

If you're average, you fart between 14 and 23 times a day. If you fart more than that, here are two things you might want to know.

Your stomach produces gas when it digests food. That's why there are two types of farts: stinky ones and odorless ones. The stinky ones smell bad because of sulfur gas that's released after you eat certain foods. Cheese and meat have a lot of sulfur in them, so those farts are more likely to smell. Beans can make you really gassy, but most of them don't have much sulfur. So bean farts don't usually smell too bad. (Of course, if you add a lot of cheese to your beans, it's another story.)

. . . .

RECORD BREAKERS

Tiana Walton, 9, from Cheshire, England, broke the record for "most snails sitting on a human face." A grand total of 25 slimed around Walton's face for 10 seconds, outpacing the previous record of 15 snails.

Yay! Rats!

Each answer contains the word RAT, so we've drawn a rat where those three letters go. Fill in the rest of the letters to answer each clue. For example, the first one is BRAT.

1. Badly behaved kid: ___

2. G, PG or PG-13: ___ ___ ___

3. Hole in the moon made by a meteorite: ___ ___ ___

4. The ___ Kid (a movie): ___ ___ ___

5. Robber at sea with an eye patch: ___ ___ ___

6. Use your nails on an itch: ___ ___ ___

7. A baby's noisy, shaking toy: ___ ___

8. What "O" on a phone stands for: ___ ___ ___

9. 26-mile running race: ___ ___ ___

10. Opposite of a Republican: ___ ___ ___

Extra Credit:

11. Focus and think hard: ___ ___ ___ ___

Answers

· · · · · · · · · · · ·

Yay! Rats!

1. brat

2. rating

3. crater

4. The Karate Kid

5. pirate

6. scratch

7. rattle

8. operator

9. marathon

10. Democrat

11. concentrate

Ogre Drool

Can you find the one path from this slobbery ogre to the mop?

Answers

Ogre Drool

Run with the Pack

There are some very creative names for groups of animals. Can you guess them?

1. What do you call a group of HIPPOS?

a. blob
b. bloat
c. flotilla

2. What do you call a group of OTTERS?

a. mischief
b. romp
c. giggle

3. What do you call a group of RHINOS?

a. army
b. platoon
c. crash

4. What do you call a group of APES?

a. meeting
b. shrewdness
c. mob

5. What do you call a group of GIRAFFES?

a. rise
b. tower
c. stand

6. What do you call a group of TIGERS?

a. ambush
b. growl
c. gang

7. What do you call a group of ZEBRAS?

a. pattern
b. herd
c. dazzle

8. What do you call a group of SQUIRRELS?

a. scurry
b. scramble
c. run

Dino-Score

Hold the book so this page lies flat. Sit up straight and hold a hand behind your head with your pinky finger sticking out. Close your eyes, bring your hand over your head and down to this page. What did your pinky land on?
Mark down the score and repeat five times.

Answers

. . . .

Run with the Pack

1. b. bloat

2. b. romp

3. c. crash

4. b. shrewdness

5. b. tower

6. a. ambush

7. c. dazzle

8. a. scurry

Crocodile Tears and Rabbit Ears

We're happy as a clam to offer up 24 animal metaphors.

BIRD BRAIN

BUSY AS A BEE

CAT'S PAJAMAS

CLOTHES HORSE

CROCODILE TEARS

CROWS FEET

DARK HORSE

DOG TAGS

EAGER BEAVERS

HAPPY AS A CLAM

HOG THE ROAD

HOLY MACKEREL

HORSING AROUND

JUDAS GOAT

KILLER BEES

MAD AS A WET HEN

MY GOOSE IS COOKED

NONE OF YOUR BEESWAX

PUT ON THE DOG

RABBIT EARS

SCAREDY CAT

SLY AS A FOX

SNAKE EYES

TURTLE NECK

```
P C K J N U T A C Y D E R A C S D M O T D
L T Y S R A E T E L I D O C O R C I P Y E
B B I R D B R A I N A E D Q I E T V M K K
N W E V A Y Z K I O S F N T Y V D R S L O
X R Y S I B Z R R C A O U W Y A L I V Q O
Q L F C R R B E I E S R O H S E H T O L C
Y Z N G O O H I S G T V R Q T B W V B T S
L G S A G T H M T L U M A B E R A D O Z I
E M H X G E P K E E A U G U E E K A E I E
R G R O S G L N R L A V N S F G P N J T S
E E H Z P C E K C A W R I Y S A U G K N O
K H Q F V C Z A M A D A S A W E T H E N O
C T U V K O S Y V O H N R S O K O I G M G
A E D E K A P L G K A L O A R K N D F D Y
M F R B Y A E T Y K J S H B C V T U G N M
Y V Q P G H A W E A H Z A E I W H R E L N
L Y P J K G E E H O S S E E B R E L L I K
O A E M S Q Y X G A T A O G S A D U J Y I
H X A W S E E B R U O Y F O E N O N X T D
G C A T S P A J A M A S V O E T G R B F U
H P U C U G T W I L P I R C X U W U X I L
```

TINGUE TWUSTERS!

Big bad bedbugs bug bigger bedbugs to beg big beds from even bigger bedbugs!

Q: What is a female polar bear's favorite state?

A: I don't know, Alaska!

Answers

· · · · · · · · · · · · ·

Crocodile Tears and Rabbit Ears

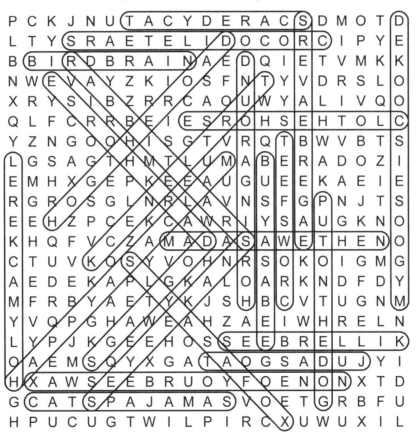

```
P C K J N U T A C Y D E R A C S D M O T D
L T Y S R A E T E L I D O C O R C I P Y E
B B I R D B R A I N A E D Q I E T V M K K
N W E V A Y Z K I O S F N T Y V D R S L O
X R Y S I B Z R R C A Q U W Y A L I V Q O
Q L F C R R B E I E S R O H S E H T O L C
Y Z N G O O H I S G T V R Q T B W V B T S
L G S A G T H M T L U M A B E R A D O Z I
E M H X G E P K E E A U G U E E K A E I E
R G R O S G L N R L A V N S F G P N J T S
E E H Z P C E K C A W R I Y S A U G K N O
K H Q F V C Z A M A D A S A W E T H E N O
C T U V K O S Y V O H N R S O K O I G M G
A E D E K A P L G K A L O A R K N D F D Y
M F R B Y A E T Y K J S H B C V T U G N M
Y V Q P G H A W E A H Z A E I W H R E L N
L Y P J K G E E H O S S E E B R E L L I K
O A E M S Q Y X G A T A O G S A D U J Y I
H X A W S E E B R U O Y F O E N O N X T D
G C A T S P A J A M A S V O E T G R B F U
H P U C U G T W I L P I R C X U W U X I L
```

Draw Rollo & Bob

Follow the steps in order. Sketch in pencil first. When you're happy with your sketch, trace over your lines in ink. Let the ink dry, then erase the pencil lines.

1.   2.   3.   4.

5.   6.

1.   3.   4.

2.

Draw a Rollo & Bob Comic Strip

Add Rollo and Bob to these four comic-strip panels. Are they standing, walking, sitting? Are they close up or far away? What are they doing with their arms?

Rollo, why is that alligator wearing a vest?

He's an investigator.

Bob, what's that fly doing in the toilet?

Looks like the breaststroke.

Come up with your own jokes for these two panels:

Uncle John's

FOR KIDS ONLY!

A Filling Joke

Fill in the name of each item below. When you're done, place each of those words in the boxes on the next page so that the yellow squares match up. There's only one way they'll all fit.

Finally, read DOWN the yellow column to find the joke's answer.

G	H	O	S	T

Why did the monster eat only the candles on his birthday cake?

G	H	O	S	T

Answers

· · · · · · · · · · · · ·

A Filling Joke

ghost, bag, cookie, ladder, butterfly, stamp, bat, pillow, hat, brush, truck, spider, nest, fish, wave, camera

Joke answer: He was a light

Myth-Conceptions

A lot of the things you may have been told just aren't true.

Myth: In the original fairy tale, Cinderella's slippers were made of glass.

Truth: Actually, they were made of fur. The goof comes from a poor translation—someone interpreted the French word vair, which means "fox fur," as verre, which means "glass."

Myth: Ninjas wore all black.

Truth: When movies and TV shows started showing ninjas—secret agents in old Japan—they borrowed the details from 19th-century Japanese plays, which put ninjas in black clothing because it looked mysterious and dramatic onstage. In reality, ninjas wore dark blue at night to fade into the dark. During the day, they wore whatever clothes they needed to blend in with crowds.

Q: What do sea monsters eat?

A: Fish and ships.

Q: What did the judge say when the skunk walked into the court-room?

A: "Odor in the court!"

Polo Shirts

Which two of Marco's shirts are exactly the same?

What do you call Marco Polo when he's at sea?

Water Polo.

1.

2.

3.

4.

5.

6.

7.

8.

Answers

· · · · · · · · · · · ·

Polo Shirts

3 and 8 are identical.
1 is missing a white cuff on one sleeve.
2 is missing the top button.
4 is missing a pocket.
5 is missing a belt hole.
6 is missing a white cuff on one sleeve.
7 is missing part of the collar.

Hole in One

There's something really mysterious about doughnuts. The minute you open a box of them—POOF!—they disappear.

Doughnuts have been around for centuries—scientists have even found fossilized fried dough in ancient American Indian ruins. The word first appeared in writing in 1803, when an English cookbook included a recipe for doughnuts. And in America, author Washington Irving published *A Knickerbocker's History of New York* in 1809. The book told funny stories about the city's Dutch settlers. In it, he wrote about "balls of sweetened dough, fried in hog's fat, and called doughnuts."

CAPTION THIS COMIC

Here's the picture. You add the words.

Oopsie Daisy!

Warning: Always do this experiment over a sink to make sure the floor doesn't get soaked.

What You Need

- 1 small drinking glass.

- 1 playing card from a deck of cards (make sure it's one you don't need anymore, because it will get wet!)

What To Do

Fill the drinking glass half way with water. Place the card over the top of the drinking glass. Make sure the card covers the mouth of the glass completely. Put pressure on the card with your hand and carefully turn the glass over. Once the glass is completely upside down, take your hand away from the card. Ta da! The card will stick to the mouth of the glass and the water will stay inside the glass.

How It Works

Two words: air pressure. The air around the glass pushes up against the card harder than the water inside the glass pushes down. In fact, you would need a glass of water almost 30 feet high before the water would weigh enough to push the card off the glass.

Did you know? The average (hic!) bout (hic!) of hiccups (hic!) lasts five (hic!) minutes.

Scabs on Toast

What You Need

- 2 slices of toast
- 12 to 16 raisins
- Butter or margarine
- Your favorite jam
- Band-Aid

What To Do

1. Take the raisins and rip them into scab-size pieces.

2. Spread each slice of toast with butter and jam.

3. Place the "scabs" all over the toast—and eat!

Barfing Band-Aid Prank

Now it's time to gross out a friend. Stick a raisin "scab" on the gauze part of a Band-Aid (don't let them see you do it!). Stick the Band-Aid on your arm or leg. Then tell your friend you're so hungry you could eat a scab. Watch them gag as you whip off the bandage and chow down on the scabs.

TOTAL ICK!

That dust in your room, on your desk, action figures and bookshelves? It's mostly dead skin.

Figure It Out

These two stick figures have a mystery riddle for you. Just fill in the letters to finish what the girl stick figure is saying. That will help you get the answer—and explain why they like that letter.

Which letter do stick figures like best?

Without it, we'd be...

Letter between R and T

Most common vowel in LETTER

It comes five letters after M

Middle letter of CARBUNCLE

7th letter of the alphabet

Letter that sounds like 👁

Worst grade on a report card

Letter halfway between G and O

Letter that sounds like SEA

Me, myself and ___

Letter that makes words plural

Read UP the column to complete her sentence.

Answers

Figure It Out

Their favorite letter is T, because
without it they'd be SICK FIGURES.

START

Down the Drain

Find the one route through these pipes from START to END. (You can go over joints and behind pipes.)

END

Answers

Down the Drain

Find the one route through these pipes from START to END. (You can go over joints and behind pipes.)

Play Time

Twenty-seven fun toys for kids of all ages.

ACTION FIGURES

BALLS

BARBIE DOLL

ELECTRIC TRAIN

ERECTOR SET

ETCH A SKETCH

HULA HOOP

JACK IN THE BOX

JACKS

JUMPROPE

KALEIDOSCOPE

LEGO BRICKS

LINCOLN LOGS

MARBLES

MATCHBOX CARS

NERF BALL

NEWTONS CRADLE

PICKUP STICKS

PLAY-DOH

PUZZLES

RUBIKS CUBE

SILLY PUTTY

SOLDIERS

TINKERTOYS

TOP

WHISTLE

YOYO

```
M Y H N Q W C H F T N G L Q S I V U R
R I T I N K E R T O Y S E I V Y N S K
B R E T H H M U Y D S V Q A X O I J F
V F S X U O A Z G E E N R O N Q A A S
J S R E O P D A S O L D I E R S R T P
D K O S B B Y Y Z I Z S L H W K T D D
P C T J R U E L A R Z C L E R C C Y D
J I C L B A C H L L U T L L V I I H W
E T E M A N C S T I P T U R A R R H L
U S R O I L L X K N S O M L F B T C I
B P E L Y L J S O I I Q O T P O C T N
J U M P R O P E H B B K N H X G E E C
J K K W O D Y W M G H U C C A E L K O
B C T N N E W T O N S C R A D L E S L
M I A W C I K O Y K J M T Q J G U A N
Y P R C T B O P X U S K C A J T B H L
L L A B F R E N S E L B R A M F M C O
V U B O K A L E I D O S C O P E G T G
J V J E W B A C T I O N F I G U R E S
```

BE A...CAT-FOOD TESTER!

It's a real job! Every batch of cat food needs someone to perform three quality-control tests. Test 1: Stick your face in a tub of cat food and take a big sniff. Is it fresh? Test 2: Plunge your arms in up to the elbows, feel for bony bits, and take them out. Got all the bones out? Test 3: Smear a big glob flat and prod it with your fingers to check for gristle. If it's gristle-free, you're done. (Whew!)

Did you know? Shrek, the ogre in the book by William Steig that was made into a movie by DreamWorks, got his name from the German word *schreck*, which means "fright" or a "scare."

Answers

· · · · · · · · · · · ·

Play Time

```
M Y H N Q W C H F T N G L Q S I V U R
R I T I N K E R T O Y S E I V Y N S K
B R E T H H M U Y D S V Q A X O I J F
V F S X U O A Z G E E N R O N Q A T S
J S R E O P D A S O L D I E R S R T P
D K O S B B Y Y Z I Z S L H W K T D D
P C T J R U E L A R Z C L E R C Y D
J I C L B A C H L L U T L L V I H W
E T E M A N C S T I P T U R A R R H L
U S R O I L L X K M S O M L F B T C I
B P E L Y L J S O I Q O T P O C T N
J U M P R O P E H B B K N H X G E E C
J K K W O D Y W M G H U C C A E L O
B C T N N E W T O N S C R A D L E S L
M I A W C I K O Y K J M T Q J G U A N
Y P R C T B O P X U S K C A J T B H L
L L A B F R E N S E L B R A M F M C O
V U B O K A L E I D O S C O P E G T G
J V J E W B A C T I O N F I G U R E S
```

1" />

Creepy Cures

Before modern medicine, people relied on folk remedies like these. We're glad we live now.

Toothache? Chew on a peppercorn.

Swollen Eyes? Take a live crab; remove its eyes. Put the crab back in the water and put the eyeballs on your neck.

Sore Throat? Tie nine knots in a black thread and wear it around your neck for nine days.

Snakebite? Put earwax on the bite and ask someone to say a prayer for you.

Ingrown Nail? Using a leather string, tie a lizard's liver to your left ankle. The ingrown toenail should disappear in nine days.

Shortness Of Breath? Take the lungs and liver from a fox. Chop them up into tiny pieces, mix with wine, and drink the concoction from a church bell.

Burns? Mix sheep dung with fresh goose grease and spread it on the affected area.

Freckles? Fourday-old lemon juice rubbed on the face will make them go away.

Cuts? Apply a large army ant to the cut, so that it takes hold of each side of the wound with its pincers. Cut the body off, leaving the ant's head to hold the cut together.

Super-Duper Squirter

Following the tubes from bottle to bottle, find the one way from START to END.

splurt

Start

End

Answers

Super-Duper Squirter

splurt

Start

End

How to Make a Spitball

Kids have so much to learn that sometimes grownups forget about the important things—like making spitballs. Even if you already know how to do this, here are some tips about the art of spitballing.

What You Need: Paper, of course, something not too stiff and not too soft. Notebook paper is great. (Hey, you've got plenty of that). You'll also need a lot of spit. (You've got plenty of that, too.)

What To Do

1. Tear off a square piece of paper that's two inches long and two inches wide, and crumple it into a small ball.

2. Stick that paper ball in your mouth. (Don't swallow it.) Chew it up, tenderizing it with your teeth and saliva. You're done when the paper is slimy and saturated with spit, but not quite falling apart.

3. Take it out of your mouth and reshape the paper/spit chunk into a ball by rolling it in the palm of your hand. If it doesn't stay in the ball shape, chew some more.

4. Launch it! The classic way is to put it on your thumb and flick it with your forefinger. You can also stick it into one end of a straw and blow hard in the other end. And please, whatever you do, don't shoot it at your little brother.

Mammoth Jokes

Q: Why were the mammoths kicked out of the swimming pool?
A: Because they couldn't keep their trunks up.

Q: What weighs 5 tons and has 16 wheels?
A: A mammoth on roller skates.

Q: Why did the mammoth cross the road?
A: Because there weren't any chickens in the Ice Age.

. . . .

GRAB-BAG SURPRISE

When a purse snatcher mugged an 86-year-old woman in Netley Abbey, England, he got a big surprise. The woman was walking her dog. Inside her handbag: the contents of her pooper scooper.

Picture This

Here's an easy way to draw the picture on the left. Just copy what you see in each square and—ta da!—a masterpiece!

TIP
It helps to sketch in pencil first.

Finish in ink, erase the pencil lines, and color.

Did you know? In China, September 20th is "Love Your Teeth Day."

Hairstory

Orange and blue hair? Old-fashioned? Yep!

The First Punks

When the Saxons invaded Britain 2,500 years ago, they went to battle with hair and beards dyed orange, green, bright red, and blue. Why? To scare the enemy. In case that didn't work, they also carried two-handed battle-axes that could cut a horse in half.

The Red Queen

Back in the late 1500s, Queen Elizabeth I's red hair sent the English into a hair-dyeing frenzy. Men and women of the court wanted to show their loyalty to the queen. So they dyed their hair (some men even dyed their beards) to match the queen's hair color. Loyalty came with side effects. The dye they used—a mix of saffron and sulfur powder—caused nausea, headaches, and nosebleeds.

Where do pilots dye their hair?

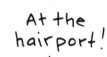

Daring Hair

After you get your parents' permission, try these wacky ways to color your hair

Tea: To tint hair red, rinse it with tea made from rose hips or Red Hibiscus.

Potato Water: To darken hair, boil unpeeled potatoes. Let the water cool, and then use it to rinse your hair.

Food Coloring: Put colorful highlights in blond hair using food-coloring paste. Separate out a strand, coat it with paste, and then cover with foil. Leave on for an hour, or overnight for more vivid color.

Washable Markers: Choose a marker and use it to highlight strands of hair. Color washes out in one shampoo.

At the hairport!

CAPTION THE COMIC

Here are the pictures. You add the words!

Woof!

klonk!

It's a Zoo in Here!

Identify each animal, then write the word in the proper spot on the next page, one letter per box. We put in ELK at 3-Down to get you started.

Across

Down

Bonus: Unscramble the letters in the yellow boxes to answer this joke: What animal has four legs and flies?

Answers

It's a Zoo in Here bonus: PIG

Stop Time? (It's Science!)

How do we know these magic tricks will amaze and delight your friends? Because we can read their minds!

The Trick: Find an old wind-up wristwatch and show your audience that it's a working, ticking watch. Then place it on a table and use your magical powers to make it stop ticking.

How It Works: Use a table with a tablecloth. Hide a magnet under the tablecloth. When you put the watch on top of the magnet, it will stop the watch. (Warning: Be sure your watch is an old, cheap one—when you remove the magnet, it will start ticking again, but sometimes the trick affects the watch's ability to tell accurate time.)

CHICKEN RIDDLES

Q: Why did it take so long for the elephant to cross the road?

A: Because the chicken had trouble carrying him.

Q: On which side does a chicken have the most feathers?

A: The outside.

Disgusting Defenses

These amazing, bizarre, and gross defense mechanisms help animals avoid becoming lunch.

Turkey Vultures can eat the nastiest, stinkiest dead animals without getting sick. While they're busy dining on the dead, it's easy for predators to sneak up behind them. If that happens, a turkey vulture will hack up undigested meat as an offering: Here, eat this instead of me!

The Texas Horned Lizard spooks predators by squirting blood from the corners of its eyes. It can shoot up to one-third of its blood a distance of more than three feet. All of that spewing gore confuses the attacker and gives the lizard time to flee.

Fulmar Gulls got their name (which means "foul gull") because of the oily yellow vomit they yack up on other birds. At just four days old, fulmar chicks can puke on predators up to 18 inches away from the nest. The vomit turns the invading bird's feathers into a sticky mess so that it can't fly. Sometimes the invader falls right out of the sky.

Draw all three!

Vulture	Lizard	Gull

Bug Sudoku

These puzzles use four different bugs. Complete each puzzle by drawing bugs in the blank squares. There's only one way to do it following these rules:

Each row must include all four bugs →

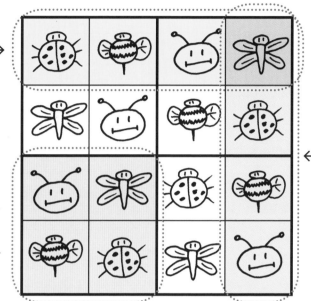

← **Each column must include all four bugs**

Each large square (with the bold lines) must include all four bugs →

2.

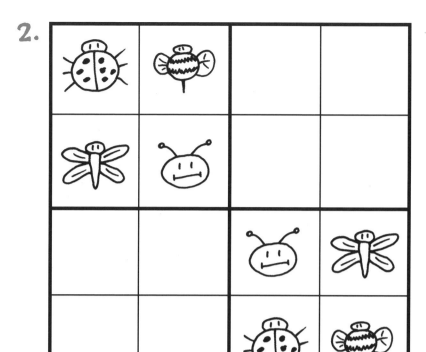

1.

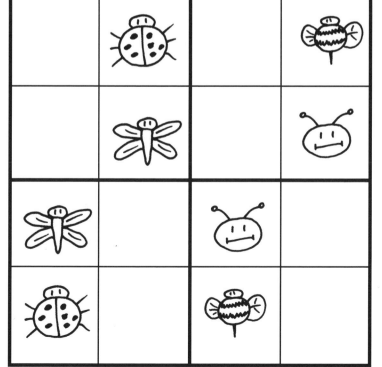

Hint:
Look at the top row. It's missing a dragonfly and a bug head. Since there's already a dragonfly in the lefthand column (going down), only a bug head can go in the upper left square.

3.

Answers

Bug Sudoku

1.

2.

3.

That's Creepy!

- Frogs use their eyeballs to push food down their throat.
- A housefly's tastebuds are in its feet.
- The jaws of a snapping turtle can keep snapping for a day after the turtle's head has been cut off.
- Snails have teeth.

· · · · · · · · · ·

GET TONGUE TANGLED

Say it three times fast—if you can!

Girl gargoyle, guy gargoyle.

HORRIBLE HUMOR

Q: What do you say to an ogre who eats your cheese?

A: Hey! That's nacho cheese!

Rotting Flesh

· · · · · · · · · · · · · · ·

Become a zombie without that icky smell.

What You Need

- 1/2 cup oatmeal
- 1 tablespoon flour
- Bowl
- Spoon
- Red food coloring
- Green food coloring

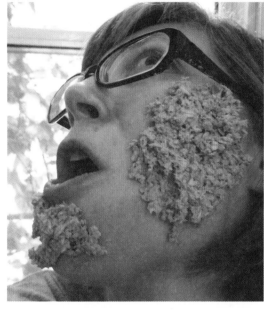

What To Do

1. Combine the oatmeal, two tablespoons of water, and one drop each of red and green food coloring in a small bowl. Stir the mixture, adding more water if needed to make a thick paste. (If the paste gets too thin, thicken it with a small amount of flour.)

2. Drip in more food coloring if you want your flesh to look especially bloody or gangrenous.

The Prank: Smear generous amounts of the oatmeal "flesh" on your face. Give it a few minutes to dry, then sneak up behind your victim and start moaning.

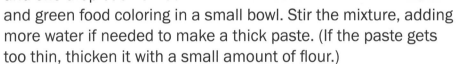

Fairy Dusting

This pixie has been hard at work sweeping up the fairy dust in the basement of her tree house. Can you trace the path she swept from START to END?

Start

End

Answers

A Dash of Salt

NaCl is the chemical symbol for salt. Use one N, one A, one C, and one L to complete *each pair* of words.

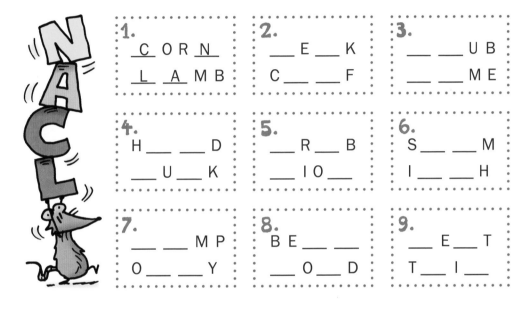

1.
_C_ O R _N_
_L_ _A_ M B

2.
__ E __ K
C __ __ F

3.
__ __ U B
__ __ M E

4.
H __ __ D
__ U __ K

5.
__ R __ B
__ I O __

6.
S __ __ M
I __ __ H

7.
__ __ M P
O __ __ Y

8.
B E __ __
__ O __ D

9.
__ E __ T
T __ I __

LOONY LAWS

- It's illegal to fish for whales in Nebraska.
- In Texas, it's illegal to sell your eye.
- In Charleston, SC, the fire department is legally permitted to blow up your house.

Crazy Crazes

Get out your pencil and fill in the blanks in this quiz.
RULES: You can only use letters from the phrase
THOSE MAD CRAZES WILL NEVER STOP.

1. In 1992 the Video Phone flopped. No one wanted to pay $1,500 for a phone that would let them see their friends with bed __ __ A __ .

2. The ad for the first movie in Smell-O-Vision said, "First they moved! Then they talked! Now they __ M __ __ L ."

3. In the 1960s, American kids went crazy for wild-haired, naked, pot-bellied dolls called T __ __ __ L __ .

4. A Swedish doctor created a way for people to lose weight: Eat like a __ __ V __ M __ __ .

5. Bit Critter, Digital Doggie, and Micro Chimp were all part of the virtual __ __ T craze that started in 1997.

6. Back in 1957, you could put your money in a pie-o-matic vending machine. What came out? __ __ Z Z __ .

7. The goopy stuff that went up and down in those lava L __ __ P __ popular in the 1960s was made from carbon tetrachloride and wax.

8. Girls danced the frug wearing __ __ P __ __ dresses, but they didn't go out in the rain!

9. Before email, kids had __ __ N pals.

Answers

A Dash of Salt

1. CORN, LAMB	6. SLAM, INCH
2. NECK, CALF	7. CAMP, ONLY
3. CLUB, NAME	8. BEAN, COLD
4. HAND, LUCK	9. CENT, TAIL
5. CRAB, LION	

Crazy Crazes

1. head	6. pizza
2. smell	7. lamps
3. trolls	8. paper
4. caveman	9. pen
5. pet	

Uncle John's
FOR KIDS ONLY!

Abominable Snow-Job?

Every region has its own name for the legendary abominable snowman.
How many can you find?

BIGFOOT (North America)

BONMANCHE (Nepal)

BUNYIP (Australia)

CADDY (North America)

EBU GOGO (Indonesia)

HIBAGON (Japan)

KAPRE (Philippines)

LOCH NESS MONSTER (Scotland)

MEHTEH (Nepal, Tibet)

MOMO (Missouri, United States)

NANDI BEAR (Africa)

OGOPOGO (Canada)

SASQUATCH (North America, Malaysia)

SKUNK APE (Florida, United States)

TESSIE (Australia)

WAMPUS CAT (Tennessee, United States)

YEREN (China)

YETI (Nepal, Tibet)

YOWIE (Australia)

Brain Buzzer

It takes a drop of newt spit

80 seconds to evaporate under a hot lamp when the mad scientist is wearing her white lab coat. When she doesn't wear the coat, it takes a minute and 20 seconds. Why is this? (The amount of spit and heat are identical.)

```
I U H        J N C B
F X E        X O Y O
R J T        H G W G
U A H        N A K Y
A E J          B C
J M B A T E I T Q M H W O
  P P I V H H E B U G O G O
    D C C P L E     M O M
    A N T A O B       P W
    V A A K C T       O S
    V M U N H Y       G W
    V N Q U N T     H O F
    S O S K E K     F F
      B A S S
      P S F S
      R I U M M W
    E E Y     O A T
    I V N     N M O
    W Q U     S P O
    O C B     T U F
    Y A G     E S G
    E D O     R C I
    R D       A B
  I T E Y     T V F G
  B X N Y     B K D K
```

Answers

· · · · · · · · · · · ·

Brain Buzzer

Because the amount of time is the same:
1 minute (60 seconds) + 20 seconds = 80 seconds.

Abominable Snow-Job?

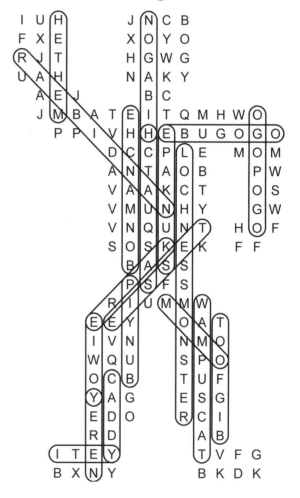

Drive Your Teacher Nuts

Making trouble in class is an old tradition—students have been doing it for hundreds of years. A few of those time-honored techniques (and some creatures to make your teacher shriek) are hidden in the schoolhouse-shaped puzzle to the right.

ARM FARTING	GARLIC	SILLY NOTES
BUBBLE GUM	ITCHING POWDER	SNAKES
BUGS	NEWT	SPIDERS
COMIC BOOKS	PRANKS	WHISPERING
FAKE EYEBALLS	PUPPY	WORMS
FERRET	SALAMANDER	YO-YO

```
                    D
                  C X M
                V O R U B
              D B M E G C X
            C S R I D E T G B
          X C P B C W L K X S B
        S M Y C Q B O B S E L Q E
      Z Z B U G S O P B C I L R A G
    D D G Z O R I O G U U S A E R N H
  C H B     H L K N B P K B D M I M
  V U E       J L S I N A P E N F R T
  F P T O Y O Y M H       Y A A E E
  B R A E H Q N R C       E M R P Z
  G A G D R B O O T       E A T S Q
  P N Z T Y R T W I       K L I I H
  V K S P I D E R S       A A N H M
  M S E K A N S F D       F S G W G
```

The Body Bizarre

These facts about your body may be hard to believe. But they're true!

• Your mouth makes enough saliva in your lifetime to fill not just one, but two swimming pools!

• There are two kinds of earwax: wet and gooey, or dry and flaky. Wet earwax is useful for trapping insects that try to sneak into your ears. But if your ears have the wet kind, you have smellier armpits.

WILD & WOOLLY WORDY

Can you figure out what word or phrase this stands for?

↓

END

Answers

· · · · · · · · · · · ·

Drive Your Teacher Nuts

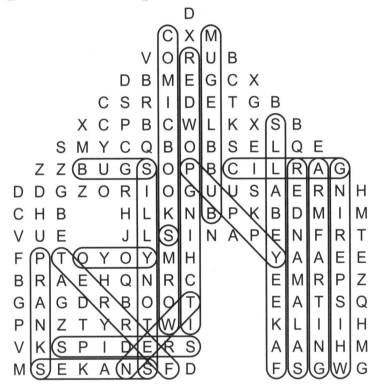

Wild & Woolly Wordy

Beginning of the end

Uncle John's
FOR KIDS ONLY!

Woof! Meow!

Each dog or cat has a name that matches what it looks like or what it's doing. Can you figure out who's who? For example, a dog with a fishing pole would be named Rod.

1. ART 2. CAROL 3. CLIFF 4. DAISY 5. SPIKE
6. PEARL 7. RICH 8. ROCKY 9. SANDY 10. JOY

DO-IT-YOURSELF:
Try drawing a dog or cat with a name that fits. Dot? Fanny? Jack? Lance? Lincoln? Peg? Use the back of the placemat if you need more room.

A. ___

B. ___

C. ___

D. ___

E. ___

F. ___

G. ___

H. ___

I. ___

J. ___

YiPPee!

Fa la la la la

Xmas Songs

Answers

Woof! Meow!

A. 6 B. 1 C. 5 D. 2 E. 7

F. 8 G. 4 H. 10 I. 9 J. 3

Uncle John's
FOR KIDS ONLY!

The Royal Sillies

Sometimes you have to be a bit bonkers to rule a kingdom. Or maybe just refuse to grow up.

• Think you hate baths? King Louis XIV of France (1638–1715) never took a bath. Not one. Ever.

• King Philip V of Spain (1683–1746) thought he would die if he changed his clothes. So he didn't. Instead, he wandered around his palace in rotting rags. He thought the tattered clothes were the only things holding him together.

• The castle built by King Ludwig II (1845–86) in his Bavarian kingdom inspired Disney's Sleeping Beauty Castle. Castles cost a lot of money. To pay for his, Ludwig planned a few bank robberies. When that didn't work, he tried to sell Bavaria. His ministers put him under house arrest to keep him out of trouble.

LIFE IN POTTERLAND

"I once played a trick on the makeup people. I put a fake-blood capsule in my mouth, and then pretended to trip on the stairs and let the blood pour out. They really fell for it! Then they chased after me with a water pistol."

—Daniel Radcliffe (Harry Potter)

A-Mazing Lipstick

Traveling on the lipstick lines, find a route from START to END.

Answers

A-Mazing Lipstick

Word Puzzles
••••••••••

1. wear
   long

2. r
   e
   t
   t
   a
   B

3. eggs
   easy

4. me snack al

5. pains

6. arrest
   you're

7. time time

8. everything
   pizza

GORILLA MANIA

Yikes! Goriillas have taken over your town.
Draw their antics in the space below.

IF YOU DARE!

Knock-knock!
Who's there?
Lettuce.
Lettuce who?
Lettuce in and
you'll find out.

Gorillas

*It's time you knew more about gorillas
than they know about you!*

• Young gorillas like to play games like Follow the Leader and King of the Mountain.

• Gorillas laugh when they're tickled and cry when they're sad or hurt.

• Gorillas are mainly vegetarians, although insects make up 1–2% of their diet. They don't seem to drink anything at all—observers think they get their water from the plants they eat.

• Gorillas support their weight on their knuckles when they walk on all fours (unlike monkeys, who use the palms of their hands).

• There can be as many as 30 gorillas in a troop.

• Every gorilla troop has a leader, a larger older male known as a "silverback" because of the gray-silver hair on his back. He makes all the decisions for the troop—and will defend it to the death.

• Adult male gorillas are about 5'6" when they stand up straight.

• The mountain gorilla is an endangered species; fewer than 400 are left in the wild.

Answers

· · · · · · · · · · · ·

Word Puzzles

1. Long underwear.

2. Batter up!

3. Eggs over easy.

4. Between-meal snack.

5. Growing pains.

6. You're under arrest.

7. Time after time.

8. Pizza with everything on it.

Potter-mania!

Everyone's favorite boy wizard stars in a puzzle even a muggle can do.

ALCHEMY

CATS

CENTAUR

DEATH
EATERS

DRACO

DUMBLEDORE

FANTASY

FAWKES

GIANT

GOBLIN

GRIPHOOK

GRYFFINDOR

HAGRID

HARRY
POTTER

HEDWIG

HERMIONE
GRANGER

HOGWARTS

HOKEY

HUFFLEPUFF

J K ROWLING

LIGHTNING
SCAR

LUNA

MAGIC

MUGGLES

NEVILLE

OWLS

POMONA
SPROUT

POTIONS

QUIDDITCH

RAVENCLAW

RON WEASLEY

SEVERUS
SNAPE

SIRIUS BLACK

SQUIBS

SYBILL

THESTRAL

UNICORN

VOLDEMORT

WINKY

WIZARDS

```
T N L N K V F A W K E S I H W R A R H G R
Y H Z A J G S O N Z N J G E A P W O K D E
E R E E N D H S Q U I B S I V G G R I S O
L S M S R E U Z N T L Y K N I W R H C L Z
S N Y A T R V M T R B F Y F A E S I H K A
A O Z L K R U I B I O H C R L P G Z D W H
E I E C K X A A L L G C T E F A N T A S Y
W T F H W C V L T L E S I G M N I H T R Y
N O D E L H A R M N E D L N C S L K E I W
O P E M K S E L A P E B O A U S W Y K R A
R U H Y A I C D B D O C A R D U O J D C Y
K U K V P O P Y W S R M H G E R R K L E R
D L E R O L T B J I U C O E A E K O K H Z
T R O D N I F F Y R G I A N T V J O L C Q
S A H A R R Y P O T T E R O A E H H S T R
A O R A C S G N I N T H G I L S Q P J I V
T B W A L C N E V A R O U M S X P I A D B
E Y V L T C V O L D E M O R T B Q R E D I
G C A T S R E T A E H T A E D D V G O I L
P Y Y P F F U P E L F F U H S E L G G U M
R N H U G S T R S P P K I D M S M I L Q T
```

Answers

Potter-mania

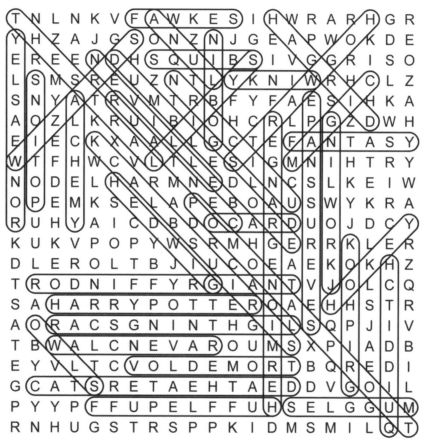

Dragon Dice

The object is to feed the dragons so they won't eat you. Do that by rolling two dice.

Let's say you roll a 3 and a 4. You could feed dragons 3 or 4—or dragon 7 (the dice total). If you roll doubles, you can feed ANY dragon.

Play with others, taking turns. Write your initials on a dragon to show you've fed it. First player to feed all the dragons wins.

No dice? Toss two coins. Feed any odd-numbered dragon if it comes up one heads and one tails. Feed any even-numbered dragon if both coins are heads. Feed no dragon if two tails are showing.

Monster Jokes

Q. Why couldn't Dracula's wife get to sleep?

A. Because of his coffin

Q. Why wasn't there any food left after the monster party?

A. Because everyone was a goblin.

Q. What monster flies his kite in a rainstorm?

A. Benjamin Franklinstein.

Q. What kind of mistakes do spooks make?

A. Boo-boos.

The Ig Nobel Prize

Who says science is boring?

Nobel? Not!

You may have heard of Nobel prizes. They're very serious awards for very serious research. But since 1991, a group called Improbable Research has awarded prizes to scientists whose work is...a bit odd. Or, as the award presenters explain, research "that first makes you laugh, and then makes you think."

2001 Biology Prize

A Colorado inventor created underwear that removes the bad smell from farts before they can escape.

2007 Medicine Prize

Doctors conducted studies to find out if sword swallowing can cause sore throats, chest pains, or stomach bleeding. The findings: Yes, yes it can.

2008 Biology Prize

French biologists found that fleas that live on dogs can jump higher than fleas that live on cats.

2010 Engineering Prize

Scientists from England and Mexico worked together to create a way to collect whale snot. They used a remote-controlled helicopter.

Mystery Joke

There's a joke below. Can you figure out how to read it? When you do, you should be able to find the answer as well.

Answers

· · · · · · · · · · · ·

Mystery Joke

Hold the bottom of the page just below your eyes and look up the page. That will shorten the letters so you can read the joke: WHY WAS THE SAND WET.

Read the same way from the right side to find this answer: BECAUSE THE SEA WEED.

Beady-eyed

Find your way through this twisting necklace of beads and beady-eyed charms.

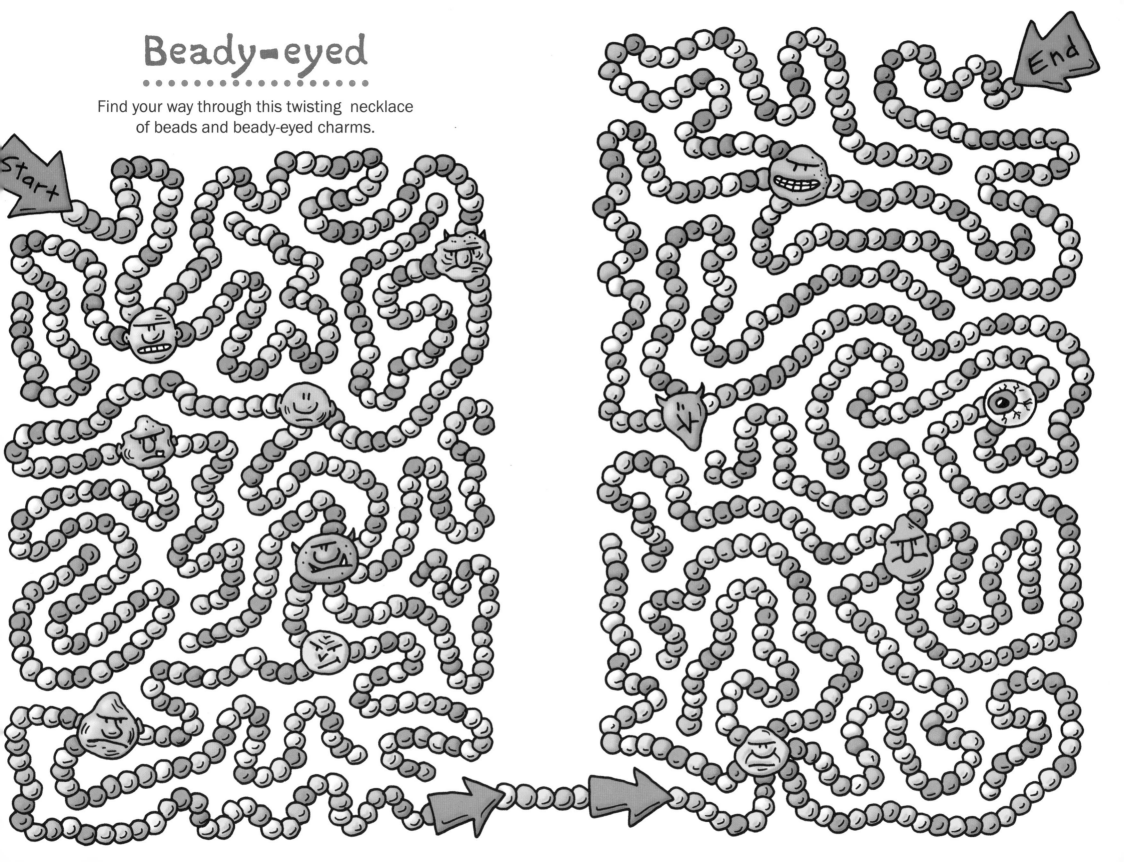

Answers

Beady-eyed

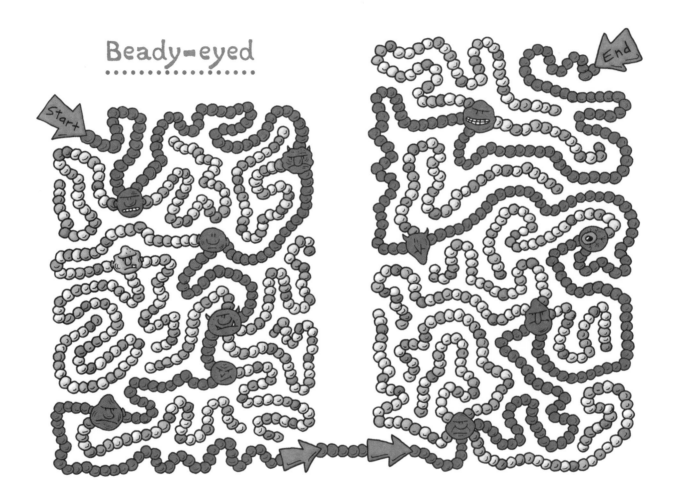

The Scoop on Poop

Plug your nose and take this quiz.

1. Which of these is not a word for outhouse?

a. Bog house

b. Necessary

c. The Drop Zone

2. Which of these three deadly diseases can be caused by water or food contaminated with poo?

a. *Escherichia coli*

b. Polio

c. Typhoid

3. The Roman god Sterculius was the

a. God of door handles

b. God of dung

c. God of ravioli

4. In the 1500s, how often did British parents change their babies' diapers?

a. Once every few days

b. Three times a day

c. When the baby pooped

5. How much did it cost to use the first public flush toilets?

a. A dime

b. A penny

c. Nothing

6. *Coleoptera scarabaeidae* is another name for:

a. The evil weevil

b. The dung beetle

c. The chicken-dung fly

7. Who was named the first head of New York City's Department of Street Cleaning?

a. George Waring

b. Thomas Crapper

c. Mr. Clean

8. Before toilet paper, people used

a. A sponge on a stick

b. Pages from books

c. Coconut husks

Making a Beeline

Starting and ending at the hive, find a path that visits every flower just once without traveling along the same dotted line twice.

Pollination: Bees help create lots of the foods we love. While collecting pollen to make their honey, bees move pollen from one plant to another, fertilizing it. Many tasty things are created that way, including cherries, watermelons, cashews, almonds, peanuts, mustard, carrots, celery, and cocoa. Yum!

Answers

The Scoop on Poop

1. C. Both "bog house" and "necessary" are terms for an outdoor toilet in Britain.

2. All three answers are correct. These three diseases, plus others such as cholera and dysentery, can be caused by contamination from feces—that's another word for poo. Such diseases have killed more people than all the wars in the history of the world.

3. B. The weird thing is that the Romans really had a god for door handles, too: Cardea.

4. A. But at least they were a step up from the moss and leaves once used to clean babies' bottoms.

5. B. The first public flush toilets were at the Crystal Palace exhibition in London's Hyde Park in 1851. An inventor named George Jennings installed "halting stations" with flush toilets for park visitors, and 800,000 people paid a penny apiece to use them.

6. B. We made up the evil weevil, but the chicken-dung fly is a real insect. Guess where it hangs out?

7. A. Before Waring took over, 2.5 million pounds of manure ended up on New York City streets every day.

8. All three answers are (painfully) correct. Sponge on a stick (Ancient Rome); pages from books (British lords); coconut husks (Hawaii).

Making a Beeline

Seeing Is Believing

Or is it? Remember—not everything is as it seems. You'll find the solutions on the next page.

Optical Illusion

The challenge: Can you tell which diagonal line on the left matches up with the diagonal line on the right?

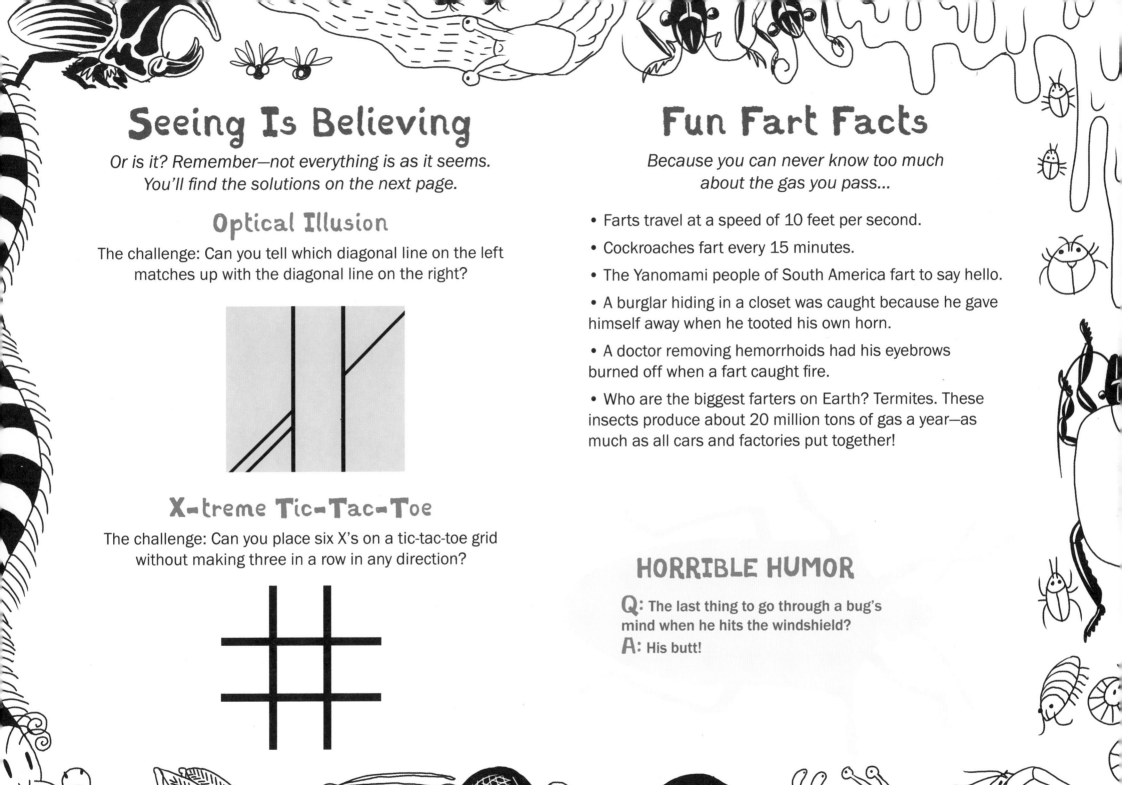

X-treme Tic-Tac-Toe

The challenge: Can you place six X's on a tic-tac-toe grid without making three in a row in any direction?

Fun Fart Facts

Because you can never know too much about the gas you pass...

- Farts travel at a speed of 10 feet per second.
- Cockroaches fart every 15 minutes.
- The Yanomami people of South America fart to say hello.
- A burglar hiding in a closet was caught because he gave himself away when he tooted his own horn.
- A doctor removing hemorrhoids had his eyebrows burned off when a fart caught fire.
- Who are the biggest farters on Earth? Termites. These insects produce about 20 million tons of gas a year—as much as all cars and factories put together!

HORRIBLE HUMOR

Q: The last thing to go through a bug's mind when he hits the windshield?
A: His butt!

Answers

· · · · · · · · · · · ·

Seeing Is Believing

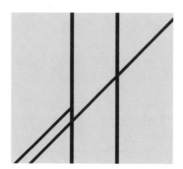 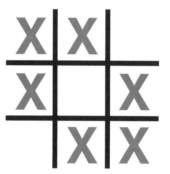

Treehouse Maze

Get from the jungle floor to the treehouse.

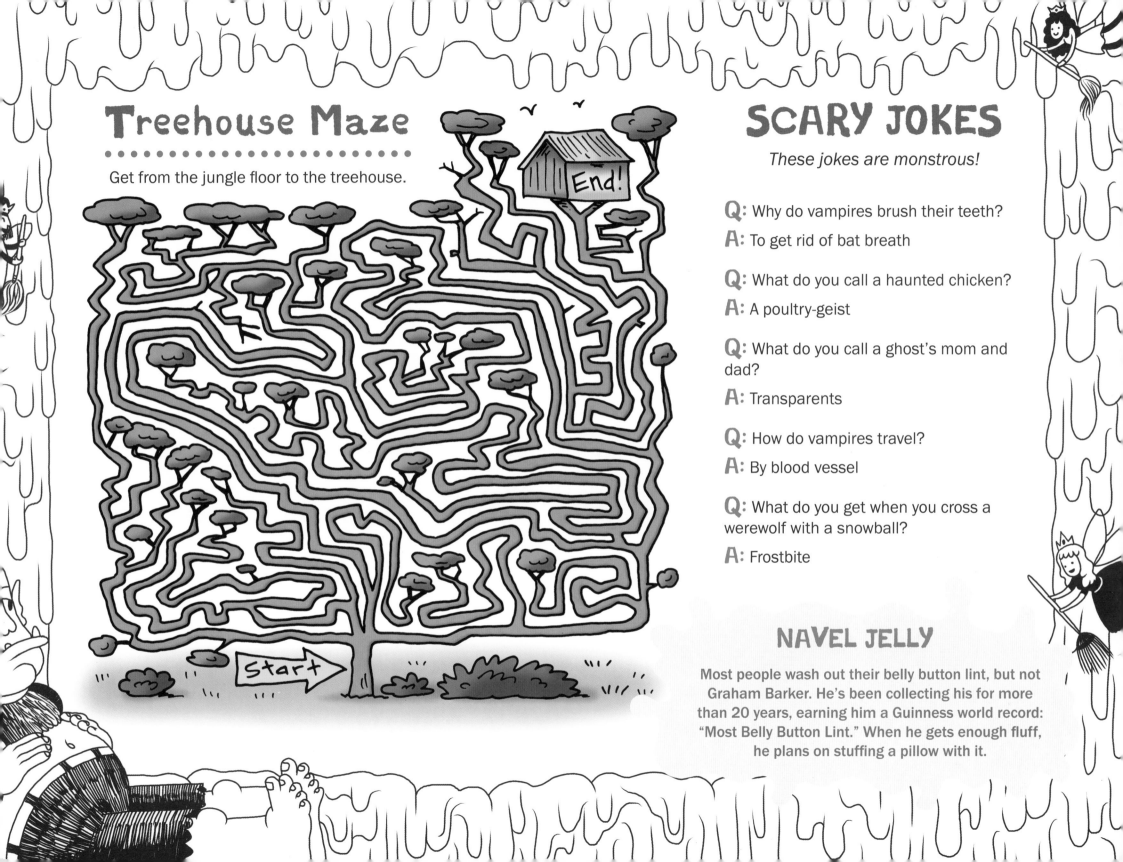

End!

Start

SCARY JOKES

These jokes are monstrous!

Q: Why do vampires brush their teeth?

A: To get rid of bat breath

Q: What do you call a haunted chicken?

A: A poultry-geist

Q: What do you call a ghost's mom and dad?

A: Transparents

Q: How do vampires travel?

A: By blood vessel

Q: What do you get when you cross a werewolf with a snowball?

A: Frostbite

NAVEL JELLY

Most people wash out their belly button lint, but not Graham Barker. He's been collecting his for more than 20 years, earning him a Guinness world record: "Most Belly Button Lint." When he gets enough fluff, he plans on stuffing a pillow with it.

Answers

· · · · · · · · · ·

Treehouse Maze
· · · · · · · · · · · · · · ·

Splash Match

Can you find the two water splashes that are identical in size and shape?

Answers

Splash Match

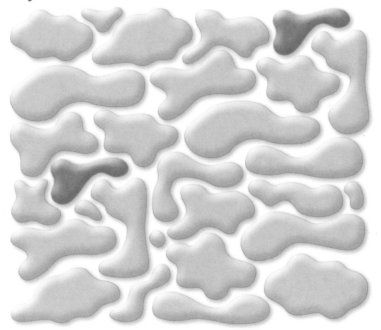